Title: Leave Early. And if you can't...?

Author: Bruce Dudon

ISBN 978-0-6458923-2-1

©2023 Bruce Dudon

PB Publishing

Gisborne | Victoria

www.pbpublishing.com.au

Printed in Australia

A catalogue record for this book is available from the National Library of Australia

Acknowledgements

Support helps, sometimes in unexpected ways, often simply inspiring ideas, and while some of those mentioned will deny all knowledge or have forgotten me and what I have been trying to do, I will still make mention of them because of their advice and encouragement.

Dave Allen CFA, Pip Butler editor, Karen Curnow, Virginia Trioli, Rosie Greenfield, Professor John Handmer RMIT, Roger Jones former Director of AEMI, Heather Knight, Ian Large, Professor Jim McLennan La Trobe University, Lawry Mahon Victoria University, Lewis Yarlupurka O'Brien a Kaurna Elder of Adelaide Plains and Honorary Fellow of the University of South Australia, Professor Tarquam McKenna Victoria University, Dr Jill Sanguinetti Victoria University and Jahne Hope-Williams.

Preface

"...in 1770 when Lieutenant James Cook, HMS Endeavour, saw something remarkable along Australia's east coast: the trees had 'No underwood.' On 1 May he 'made excursion into the country which he found diversified woods, lawns and marshes; the woods are free from underwood of every kind and trees are at such a distance from one another that the whole country or at least a great part of it might be cultivated without being obliged to cut down a single tree."[1]

If we love our country, we must be prepared to learn how it works. The 1939 Streeton Royal Commission stated the need to educate us on how to prepare for fire, flood, and other disasters.

Bushfire depends on fuel, heat, wind and ignition. That, along with the land and its form—hilly, mountainous, or dry desert country, will assist or inhibit the way fire moves. The 2009 Black Saturday fires in the Whittlesea district travelled ridge-top to ridge-top at such a rate as to be unstoppable.

This work is based on the Central district of Victoria. However, it will be similar in the way fire suppression is carried out in other areas. Living in the northwest of Victoria for example, will present different conditions to those in Gippsland. The details relating to your district are available from your local fire service.

---

1 Gammage, B.; 2011, *The Biggest Estate on Earth,* p5

Contents

Dedication

To all emergency workers, particularly the volunteers, who help
protect our communities while risking the loss of their own
properties. Also to the people of the first nations who chatted with
me from time to time and helped with my work.

1

Introduction

Do we need another tragedy, another 'Black Saturday'?

Bushfire is part of Australia, particularly in South-Eastern Australia.
Major fires have devastated lives and now, we are encouraged to
'Leave Early'. In 2003 the Auditor General, J.W. Cameron, wrote in
the foreword to *Fire Prevention and Preparedness*: "Individual
members of our community have some of the most important
responsibilities for wildfire prevention and preparedness. Victoria's
professional and volunteer firefighters deliver outstanding service, but
ultimately the responsibility for protecting our own lives and property
from wildfire lies with each of us as individuals."[2]

After 25-plus years as a volunteer member of CFA and having
seen the outcomes of bushfire, I think we must heed the words of the
Auditor General and take some responsibility for ourselves. I attended
several meetings of the Royal Commission regarding the 2009 fires
and this work has been put together to help the community understand
why fire can be good, bad, and ugly. A Chinese proverb says, 'Tell me
and I'll forget, show me and I may remember, involve me and I will
understand.'

'Leave Early' is the cry every fire season. Why should you leave
early?

2 Cameron, J.W.; 2003, *Fire prevention and preparedness*, p.vii

To build a better understanding of bushfire and how we might be able to manage it from an individual standpoint, we need to ask: What is fire? How is it made? What is the cause? How can we stop it? When do we leave? Where can I go if in danger or uncertain of what might be? What should I do and when should I do it? How can I do it? Who can help me? And, if fire doesn't happen, what then? Many questions, with many answers.

Wherever you choose to live, you need to know how to manage in times of danger.

Christopher Zinn is a speaker for campaigns on energy and private health, and a media commentator: "Once the smoke cleared, the finger pointing really began," he said in an ABC program in 2006. Speaking about the 1939 Black Friday fires, he said, "Just two weeks after the fires, the Victorian Parliament set up a Royal Commission under the visionary Judge Leonard Stretton. Of course, there had been deadly fires in the state before but nothing on this scale, and as Stretton was later to hear, the Australian race had a weakness for burning. For the first 150 years of white history, there was a reckless culture of lighting fires in the bush. Stretton would find that most of the 1939 fires were, in his words, 'lit by the hand of man'. In a wake-up call, he found the fires sprang not from arson, but from a thoughtless acceptance that fire could be part of clearing and working in the bush. 'Almost all fires are caused by man. Settlers, miners and graziers are the most prolific fire-causing agents. Their firing is generally deliberate. All other firing is generally due to carelessness'."[3]

Yes, fire can destroy, but in time, promotes growth and improves pasture.

The Country Fire Authority in Victoria recommends that on days of total fire ban, enact your fire plan. This may include leaving early. If you are to leave early, you need to consider the needs of your family—

3 Zinn, Christopher; ABC Radio, 12 December 2006

children, the elderly, the disabled, along with pets and livestock.

Having decided to leave early, you must be prepared to stay away for days, not simply one day or overnight. If there is a fire in your area, it could be a day or more before the area is declared safe and you are able to return home. Following Black Saturday in 2009, some residents were unable to return for two weeks.

Something missing from general education is learning how to remain safe from fire. The 2009 Victorian Bushfires Royal Commission reminded us of what the Stretton Royal Commission into the 1939 fires said, "...national and regional bushfire education be delivered to all Australian children as a basic life skill, with an emphasis on preparedness and survival as well as the role of fire in the Australian landscape," raising the question, do we stay, go, or prepare carefully?[4]

Climate change is realistically part of our world and has been going on for millions of years, though vastly speeded up since the industrial revolution. I see it as an important part of the work before us. If it is hot and getting hotter, we must adapt to the seasons under which we live. We cannot keep walking away.

Finally; if we could change the way things are done, we would no longer fear flood, famine, and fire. In the words of Omar Khayyam: "... could thou and I with Fate conspire To grasp this sorry Scheme of Things entire, Would not we shatter it to bits—and then Remould it nearer to the Heart's desire!". Persian mathematician Omar Khayyam made it clear—if we want change, we can't wait on the bureaucracy. We must do it ourselves.

Bruce Dudon M Ed, Grad Cert Vocational Ed Training
Former Communications Officer Mt Macedon Fire Brigade
Group Training Officer and Crew Leader

4 2009 Victorian Bushfire Royal Commission, Final Report, 2010, p55

2

Stay or go —
Things to think about

A neighbour told me what he would do in the event of fire. "Don't worry mate, she'll be right! I'll leave if fire comes near". He lived on a road where he could go either right or left. If the fire was to the right, he would go left, and vice versa. Fire is often accompanied by strong winds and may spot to the left or right. It may have brought a large tree down, thus blocking escape.

Another thing to think about; what if you live on a No Through Road—one way in, one way out. Or if the fire starts at night and is not noticed until it is too late?

Kerry O'Brien, in his memoir, writes of the situation in St Andrews on the day. The fire "…had been filmed by a local resident, Jim Baruta, as the fire raced towards his home, travelling 10 kilometres in ten minutes—half a kilometre in 10 seconds, he said … 'The flames were just so high, I would guess about fifty metres, and the sound was just incredible, like jets coming over. It was almost deafening, like the loudest thunder you've ever heard. And then when it hit here the fire was so intense, the heat was unbearable.' Twenty-two people died in his neighbourhood."[5]

It is important to note the numbers of people who died during

5 O'Brien K, 2018, *A Memoir*, p715

4

You've chosen turning right or left;
but could high winds have felled a tree further along the road?

bushfires. This is not intended to scare you but to help you think about safety and survival. As you will see, Black Saturday was the worst in relation to deaths. The number of those injured is another story and the people suffering mentally following any of the fires mentioned, could be huge.

MAJOR FIRES AND DEATHS IN VICTORIA
since 1851

- 2009   7 February-March "Black Saturday" (173 deaths)

- 1998   2 December Linton, Western Victoria (5 deaths)

- 1997   21 January Dandenong Ranges (3 deaths)

- 1985   14 January Avoca, Central Victoria (3 deaths)

- 1983   16 February "Ash Wednesday" (47 in Victoria)

- 1977   12 February, Western Victoria (8 deaths)

- 1969   8 January (23 deaths)

- 1965   17 January Longwood, Northern Victoria (7 deaths)

- 1962   14-16 January (33 deaths)

- 1952   January-March, Central Victoria (10 deaths)

- 1944   December-February (51 deaths)

- 1943   22 December (10 deaths)

- 1942   Western Victoria (20 deaths)

- 1939   December-January "Black Friday" (71 deaths)

- 1926   14 February-March "Black Sunday" (60 deaths)

- 1905   1 December (12 deaths)

- 1898   1 February "Red Tuesday" (12 deaths)

- 1851   6 February "Black Thursday" (12 deaths)

If it is a 'No Through Road' there is only one way out;
how do you escape?

The number of homes lost is difficult to assess. However, in the Ash Wednesday and Black Saturday fires, a total of 4300 homes are known to have been destroyed. There are local refuge centres run by the local shires and councils, and while it seems a great idea, is it away from the threat? And can I take the cat and dog? Pets are very important to families.

Our bodies respond to threat in a fight or flight mode. The brain activity has been described by Dr Craig Cormick who stated, "When it comes to the fear factor, even the physical layout of our brains is working against us. Studies have shown that sensory inputs are sorted by the thalamus—sort of the brain's post office—and sent on to different parts of the brain to respond to. But the amygdala, which is the 'danger, danger…' part of the brain, is located closer to the thalamus and gets to respond to messages before any other part does, certainly a lot quicker than a response coming back from the prefrontal cortex that is responsible for our higher order of thinking and decision making."[6]

My understanding is, 'running away' does not always realise our safety because you may run when it is not safe. You may choose to seek safety at the local refuge, but will it be available or itself closed due to fire threat? These are matters to be considered when leaving home.

Adrian Hyland describes a family from the Kinglake fire during the Black Saturday fires of 2009: "By mid-afternoon they're wondering whether there's any point in leaving. They've already evacuated so many times this summer. The change can't be far off now and the internet says the fire is still at Kilmore."[7] The family escaped after the fire engulfed their home.

6 Cormick, C., ABC Radio 23 October 2011
7 Hyland, A., 2011, *Kinglake-350*, p125

3

We are staying
Late evacuation is evacuation into danger

The higher the fire danger rating, the higher the risk. Code Catastrophic is the highest and the most dangerous. If you have decided to leave, it is a good idea to LEAVE EARLY. It is important to understand when it is the right time to go, or if it is safer to stay. Recent evidence "…suggests that prepared but otherwise untrained people can protect their homes from bushfires by staying with and actively defending them."[8]

Fires can take place at any time. It does not have to be a hot summer's day. The day can be warm, say 25 degrees, with a light wind blowing. If the fuels are dry and somehow a spark lands amongst them, we might have a fire. While the conditions may seem low, a nasty blaze can be up and running. That is why we say, be prepared.

In Section 6 of the Final Report of the 2009 Royal Commission in reference to buildings; "… the report indicates that most houses are damaged by embers, rather than by direct flame contact or radiant heat; that a house is more likely to survive if people actively defend it: and in the absence of human intervention a house is likely to burn to the ground once ignited, rather than just be damaged."[9]

On a day where there is a high likelihood of fire, if you have made

8 Tibbits Amalie & Handmer John, et al; 2008, *Community Bushfire Safety*, p59
9 Point 6.1, 2009 Victorian Bushfire Royal Commission Final Report, 2010, p216

the decision to stay, it is probably too late to change your mind.

The 2009 Royal Commission noted, "...encourage people to adopt the lowest risk option available to them ... the reality is people will continue to wait and see."[10] And so, if you are staying, begin by checking the list of tasks to be carried out and assign them to the appropriate family member. Remember, be aware of what you might hear – sirens; smell – smoke; see – smoke.

First, remove the 'Welcome' door mats and store them away from the house. Next, check the pump is working — squirt some water around the ground. Half fill some buckets with water — a full bucket of water is heavy (very hard work). I do not suggest heaving full buckets of water at a fire, large or small. As a rule, the bucket thrower tends to use far too much water and extreme amounts of energy. A good idea is to use a toy water gun. You can pump it to build pressure and then squirt accurately at any sparks. Indoors, a wet house mop can be used if embers enter. Wheelie bins can be half filled with water and set up around the house. A garden rake is very useful to pull smouldering piles apart and then cool them by sprinkling with water.

If you have an electronic gate, it is a good idea to have it opened. This avoids it remaining locked if the power goes off and thereby not allowing access for a fire brigade vehicle to enter. If you hope for a fire truck to arrive, your entrance must be clear 3.5 metres in height and width, otherwise no truck, no real support. If you have decided to stay, unlock all doors and windows. This will enable entry at any time for those working outside. Have plenty of water available for those at home, not forgetting your pets.

Have you spoken with your next-door neighbours? Are they leaving early? If not, what do you know of their plans for such a day? If you know their plans and their thinking, it gives you the chance to work together in emergency situations. Share your thinking.

10 Point 1.6.2, 2009 Victorian Bushfire Royal Commission, 2010, p32

4

And now...

You have made the decision

Having decided to stay, what will you do while you wait? It's easy. You simply wait, and wait, and wait. Even if you believe the fire has passed by, and, unless there is a wind change, you won't have to wonder and wait — Or will you?

If you take the position of waiting, you must be vigilant. Are there any embers close to the house or in the gutters? What about the shed? Have we thought about where any potential threat could be lurking?

Most important, water. You need to be very aware of water for YOU. If you don't consume enough water, you will be in trouble and may not be able to work in the heat of the day. While waiting, be aware of heat stroke. Symptoms of heat stroke are heat rash, dizziness, cramping and an increase in body temperature. It is important to remain cool by drinking water, around double what you would normally drink. Avoid tea, coffee and alcohol which promote dehydration, so avoid the booze. You can devour fruit to help maintain fluid intake.

In the early stages wear lightweight clothing if indoors and have the outdoor clothing at hand. If people show signs of confusion or demonstrate obvious change, cool them down.

This is the time to be aware—the time to be checking for those glowing and/or smoking signs of fire. They may not appear until the early morning, or perhaps just as you hit the pillow, so make sure someone else takes over the watch. Then you are up and running—but not literally! Running is something you should not do! Why? Because if you trip on the hose or the other tools you laid out, you may be stopped from defending your life and home. You walk. You walk quickly and safely.

Family members will share the watch through the night, with others to take over in the morning.

Friends in the Marysville area were home during Black Saturday and saved their home by extinguishing a fire which started in the eaves.

Fires are clever things. They wait as we do, and then, when least expected, they strike. So, we must be ready.

5

Taking care...

is most important; keep on caring

The fire has passed, and a wind change is about to take place—a change that may bring the fire back towards your home. This is the time to be active—the time for refilling the fuel tank on the pump if needed and ensuring everybody is ready. You need constant patrolling of your home and other outdoor assets. Watch out for smouldering tree roots. You must maintain watch, and as much as this may seem excessive, it is you, your family, and your possessions that you are looking after.

You must retreat when the heat becomes unbearable. Go inside and take a position where you can observe all that is happening. You <u>do not wait in the bathroom.</u> Why? Many bathrooms do not have a good clear vision of what is happening outdoors and have only one door. While the smoke makes it seem impossible, you will be able to tell when the main fire has passed. Then on with the breathing mask and back to work monitoring and cooling any hot spots or flames.

If the house begins to burn, wait until it is totally unbearable and then go outside onto the burnt ground. It will be hot, but you should be safe. If you have planned and prepared well, you should be OK. Some of the people who died during Ash Wednesday remained outside in the heat of the approaching blaze whilst trying to protect their homes, which survived, and suffered the consequences. Safety must be first, second and third on your survival program.

And if the fire does not arrive? How will you feel—pleased or flattened? You have gone to all that trouble and now nothing. Worth thinking about.

6

Children

'Involve me and I will understand'

Experiencing a bushfire is a frightening experience and may lead to unexpected physical and emotional responses. "… the desire to remove children from perceived danger can be overwhelming and may result in high-risk behaviour."[11]

When a bushfire threatens, families with children are presented with individual needs and challenges. The decision to leave early with the family together, or to stay and defend with all or part of the family, is one that parents must make for themselves. However, they will need to consider the psychological impact that splitting a family may have on individual members, not forgetting the member who remains home to protect the family home.

"…when it comes to children there is an understandable tendency to think of removing them from the possibility of a home coming under ember or direct flame attack," wrote Helen Goodman and Mae Proudley (RMIT University) in 2008.[12]

A family's survival plan will also need to consider that bushfire may threaten on a school day or when the children are away from home for some other reason. Given that parents should decide what is best for their family, there does need to be a backup plan that will keep

11 Goodman, Helen and Proudley, Mae; 2008, *Community Bushfire Safety,* p47
12 ibid p55

their children safe should it become too late to leave.

Research suggests that involving children in the family's planning can help them grow up understanding bushfire emergency. Being mentally prepared may mean being less fearful. Parents can also tell their children that sometimes they feel scared as well, but having a plan helps them. Remember to use language they can understand when responding to their questions. Be positive and reassuring. Remind them that by being ready, the family can avoid being hurt in a bushfire.

"Children and youth need to be informed about the disaster in age-appropriate language. Having explained the hazards and related impacts, children and youth will need reassurance from parents ... include comforting, a lot of cuddling, verbal support and letting them know they are safe," wrote a Monash (South Africa) academic in 2023.[13]

What can children do?

If we involve children in the preparation of the property before the fire season each year, this will demonstrate their importance and how they can help the family. If you talk together, there can be a sharing of ideas and concerns, and a move towards togetherness. Children may be aware of things you cannot see or have not thought of.

Children can think about the special belongings they would want to take with them should they have to leave early. They could have a special 'fire box' with a ready-made list to pack things they have chosen.

Helping children learn important phone numbers to call in an emergency and where to find that information is very useful.

During bushfire, children may also become anxious about their friends' welfare. Parents can talk to their children about where they would feel safe should they have to leave early.

13 Babugura, Agnes A; 2012, *Children, youth and disaster*, p440

It is important to listen to what children are saying. Ask questions to find out what is concerning them. You can build their confidence and a sense of security by talking about how you have prepared and how they have helped you.

Involving children in the planning process will make them familiar with what needs to happen should a bushfire emergency arise.

Again, Agnes Babugura. "For parents, guardians and community members to effectively exercise their role when a disaster strikes, they need to be guided by the young people's best interests. ... not only will children and youth be equipped to cope with disasters and prepare before disaster strikes."[14]

Something to think about

A publication titled 'The Long Way Home', edited by Heather Knight and Catherine Turnbull, presents the recollections of those directly involved in the Black Saturday fires in the Mitchell Shire. The book includes the words of Jacqui Sims. So that Jacqui could attend to her fire preparation, she asked neighbours if her daughter, Myia, could go there and be with their children. Sometime later, "Myia ran up to me with terror on her face and I thought 'How could I have done that?' I truly believe every single person on that day made the best decision they had with information they had on hand ... I am so lucky because Myia and I were OK."[15]

*There are many websites available for information on children and bushfire, for example Bushfire CRC (Cooperative Research Centre), betterhealth.vic.gov.au and psychology.org.au/topics/disasters

14 ibid
15 Knight, Heather & Turnbull, Catherine; op cit p173

7

Mental issues
How many times will you leave?

A couple left their mountain retreat seven times during the fire season in 2009 and each time they returned, there had been no fire and their home was still there. That is good news! But the effect on them was such that they chose to move away to a larger town. Some years later, they wished to return but the cost of heading back to the original location had increased markedly. They missed the people they had shared their lives with, in the community. If you have decided to leave early on more than one occasion and fire was not at any stage threatening your part of the world, will you leave early on the next, and following, Total Fire Ban days?

In the Final Report of the 2009 Royal Commission; "They observed that trauma may not become evident for a long time, and it is often not well-recognised by the affected individual or treating medical professionals." "…people present to general practitioners … with relatively minor or unrelated medical complaints. Individuals may not understand the link between their physical symptoms and their mental state."[16]

A couple of years back, I was talking to a local, Jahne, about the Ash Wednesday fire of 1983 and learnt: "I was here on Ash Wednesday

16 Point 8.9.1, 2009 Victorian Bushfire Royal Commission, Final Report, 2010, p337

and at a recent dinner, we were talking about Black Saturday. As the conversation went on, I broke into tears and couldn't stop. The memories came flooding back. Here we are, 30 years after the fire, I am crying uncontrollably. In the next weeks, I went through a hard time with those recollections."[17]

Why do we 'hide' our fears and thoughts away? Is it because it was all so bad, we couldn't manage to think about it and so put it in a safe, secure part of the memory, to be released at the most inopportune time? It is important to consider how you might manage following a traumatic event such as fire. The memories of Helen Gibson from Ash Wednesday can help our thinking. "Don and I didn't think we had been affected, but we had. We found we were only capable of making one decision at a time. It wasn't until nearly 12 months later that we found ourselves again able to deal with more than one thing at a time," she wrote.[18]

Thoughts will hound us — Should we have stayed? Should we have left earlier? What if …? I knew we should have fixed the pump; Should we stay living in the middle of the forest … There are so many things that could affect our wellbeing mentally, as well as physically. That is why preparation is vitally important. For example, do you have enough fuel for the car or pump? Whether planning to leave early or to stay and defend, make sure you have sufficient fuel in your cars. During the Ash Wednesday fire, a resident had made his way out of Macedon and headed for Riddells Creek. "I saw I was out of petrol. Luckily there was enough in the tank to make it to the fire station, but they couldn't help…"[19]

Following Black Saturday, I met Karen Curnow and heard a little about her time during and after the fire. Karen wrote a book outlining not only what she experienced, but the mental aftermath. "In a matter of hours my carefully constructed life was reduced to rubble—a

17 Hope-Williams Jahne, personal conversation, 2015
18 Gibson, Helen, in *Memories of Ash Wednesday,* 2023, p243
19 Stafford, Mark, ibid, p113

ruthless reminder that nothing is forever and that change comes in the blink of an eye."

Karen spoke of her attempts to return to work and a normal life. "At first I felt I should be able to return to some semblance of normal … When I attempted to do just that, I felt physically sick and had to stop—my body's way of letting me know that it had no more adrenaline … and was exhausted from the whole experience.

"That choice, that decision to try to see the big picture when everything around me was in ruins, has not only allowed me to see and experience the flipside of my misfortune, but has meant that somehow, incredibly, wonderfully and finally, I have my new beginning."[20]

Another anecdote of the difficulties that may confront people after a severe fire was highlighted by Geoff Hudson on ABC radio in 2010: "… a friend who lives in Coombs Road, Kinglake … her house was burnt to the ground … She lived in a shipping container during the winter of 2009 without electricity or running water."

Why was this person forgotten and left to manage under these conditions? Were authorities aware of her situation?

20 Curnow K; 2010, *Long Way Home*, ppvii, 57, 110.

8

The disabled
People we may not be aware of

While the sick and elderly are of importance during times of threat we are also bound to support the many people in our communities who are disabled in one way or another, from poor or no eyesight to the need for physical support for wheelchair users and/or those suffering mental issues. How do we help them and what are the support systems available?

In the event of fire threatening, evacuation is the obvious way out but if friends or family members are essentially unable to manage, what can we do? People who cannot see, hear, walk or drive are potentially in a desperate situation. Unless your community is prepared to assist those with such difficulties, how will they manage on such an occasion?

In 'The Routledge Handbook of Hazards and Disaster Risk Reduction,' there are comments regarding such matters:

"Procedures and services should be accessible equally at normal times and in disaster.

"Emergency communications should be available, comprehensible and reliable.

"Where there is a significant risk of disaster, appropriate preparation, education and training should be provided for the benefit of emergency responders and people with disabilities who are at risk."[21]

If you have family or friends such as those noted, it is important they are not forgotten.

21 Alexander, D.; Gaillard J.C. and Wisner B.; 2012, *Handbook of Hazards...*, p421

9

What is fire?
Friend or foe?

Fire is that hot thing that we stand in front of when cold, barbecue our meals on, but want to avoid in summer. It is also a thing that receives a lot of media coverage, including pictures which may show only the worst of the fire. This raises an important question—a question we must try to understand in relation to where we live, work or holiday.

Fire is something that many of us know little about. It is the burning of fuel such as rubbish, grass, timber, or scrub. Scrub is comprised of weeds, fallen leaves, small bushes, and the fallen branches of bigger plants. If a high wind is blowing, a fire can become more intense and dangerous because of the presence of high fuel levels.

Simply, a bushfire day usually has very high temperatures, strong wind, low humidity, and very dry materials to feed on. Drought will increase the intensity of fire. If we remove the fuels which are the base of any fire, we can reduce the risk.

The cause of fire is varied. Lightning is a major factor, with sometimes thousands of strikes per day. While not always seen, lightning can be the thing that starts the small, hardly visible fire, hidden until it begins to move.

Many fires, for example 1983 Ash Wednesday and 2009 Black

Ground fuels.

Saturday fires, were the result of clashing power lines and/or poor maintenance of the power system.

Another cause can be a previous fire which smoulders away unnoticed and then warmer weather causes the fire to flare up. An example—a shed was destroyed by fire. The cause was found to be a burn-off conducted by the property owner earlier in the year, metres away from the shed. The fire had smouldered underground along a tree root leading to the shed. This, I believe, happened near Ballarat. Importantly it tells of possibilities.

Following the Ash Wednesday fires, the Wade family of Woodend said, "The next few weeks we spent putting out burning roots of trees, sinking inches into the burnt soil and ash..."[22]

Fires can be caused by people who are careless in the use of machinery and consequently start a fire accidentally; for example by sparks from an angle grinder. Fires can also be lit deliberately.

When people hear the term 'firestorm', what impact does it have on them?

The words appearing in the media can be, and often are, misleading. They can exaggerate the truth with headlines like 'Town has been devastated', 'Worst fires in history', 'Forests have been totally destroyed' or 'Town surrounded by fire'. A Professor of Forest

Media outlets tend to catastrophise bushfire.

22 Sharon Wade in *Memories of Ash Wednesday*, Bryan Power (ed), p278

Ecology at the University of Tasmania, David Bowman, said on the ABC's Ockham's Razor program, "Fire is destructive, fire is essential for human life and fire has a spiritual dimension. When reminded of fire's potency it is often because the media frames fire as a disaster."[23]

Not all fires are devastating, but they can still destroy property and lives.

Grass fires, while not as bad, can still cause trouble if not attended. They can spread to timbered country or simply race up to your back fence, into your garden, and next it is knocking at your door.

The loss of a home or other property is often the main outcome of a bushfire, along with the emotional effect of losing many (or all) personal items. In addition, infrastructure, pets and livestock may also be lost. The main danger of fire is severe injury or death. A bushfire can burn at a temperature of 1100 degrees if the flames are 50 metres high. Imagine if you are standing right in front of them. If you step back by 50 metres from the 1100-degree heat, the temperature you are exposed to might be nearer 300 degrees. A flame one metre high has a much lower temperature.

The extent of injury to those trying to save homes and associated belongings can be horrific. Even when you are well prepared, it is not easy to save everything. As noted earlier, people died in Victoria on Ash Wednesday whilst outside protecting their homes which, ironically, survived the fire.

Let us discover the fire fuel triangle and how it works. The apex of of the triangle are the tall trees. Many people worry about the tall trees surrounding them, particularly the eucalypts. They burn, and burn very well. Next, heading down the side of the fire triangle, come shrubs and creepers. Depending on their height, shrubs can contribute to a fire. At the base of the fire triangle are grasses, leaves and, perhaps, rubbish.

23 Bowman, David; ABC Radio, 23 July 2011

It is these small things that catch fire easily (building the heat), known as ladder fuels.

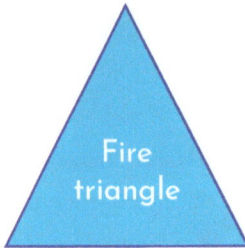

The different leves of vegetation that fuel fires and help fire move upwards are known as ladder fuels.

Here is our fire triangle—a simple ladder of how fire elevates and becomes hotter. If we remove most of the ground fuel, leaves and rubbish, we have solved problem one. You don't need to remove them totally, just keep the area tidy. Next, the shrubs and creepers. If they are reaching up into the tops of trees, it would be worth monitoring them and cutting them back if they are running wild. The main thing is to get rid of the kindling. Fire needs convection to take hot air upwards, lifting the flames with it. During a fire, if the low stuff is minimal, the fire has difficulty escalating into the trees.

When fighting a fire, many people tend to point the hose at the treetops. It is better to point the hose at the base of the triangle. The heat is reduced, and the fire slows.

In dry, windy environments, fires can spot up to 30 or 40 kilometres. This means it is important to maintain watch during local fires, or fires within these distances if the wind is heading in your direction.

10

Is it possible to stop fire?
And shape our own future?

'Yes,' is the simple answer. It can be stopped, and the sooner, the better. Fire can be stopped if reported early and brigades can attend within the first minutes.

However, fires such as the Ash Wednesday and Black Saturday outbreaks were exceptional in their speed and ferocity. These fires were caused by poorly maintained power poles and lines. The fires they started subsequently killed many people, destroyed many homes and people's future lives. "The suspected cause of the East Trentham/ Mount Macedon fire [known as the Ash Wednesday fire, 1983] was the arcing of power lines when in contact with trees," says the CFA.[24]

"The Black Saturday fire [2009] began with the Kilmore East fire when fallen power lines started a blaze in farmland at 11:47am," says the Australian Disaster Resilience Knowledge Hub.[25]

The rate of spread depends on the amount of fuel, the temperature, wind speed and humidity. On top of that, topography is an important factor. If a fire is running uphill its speed will double for every 10-degree increase in slope. Now, back to the idea of the triangle. For every 10 degrees of slope, if a fire is travelling at 5km per hour along

24 www.cfa.vic.gov.au
25 Knowledge.aidr.org.au

flat ground and it hits a 10-degree slope, it will double in speed to 10km per hour. And so, another 10 degrees it will double speed again. By increasing in speed, the fire also increases in intensity, becoming hotter because it is drying the fuels ahead.

Fig 1

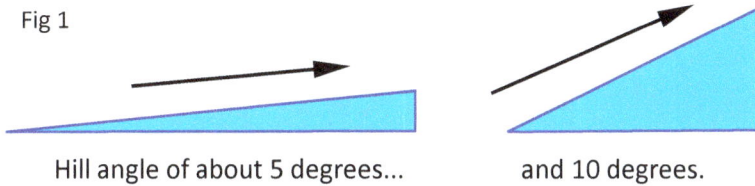

Hill angle of about 5 degrees...   and 10 degrees.

Downhill is much slower. When travelling downhill there is less radiant heat to pre-heat the fuel in front of the fire. For every 10° of downhill slope, the fire will halve its speed. Fires move more slowly as the slope decreases.

Then the cool change comes along bringing relief—or does it? When a fire is heading north to south and has a relatively small front, it is important it can be stopped. Once the cool change arrives in southern Victoria, the wind swings 90 degrees, meaning the former 10-kilometre fire with a 500-metre head, becomes a 10-kilometre front or head.

Fig 2

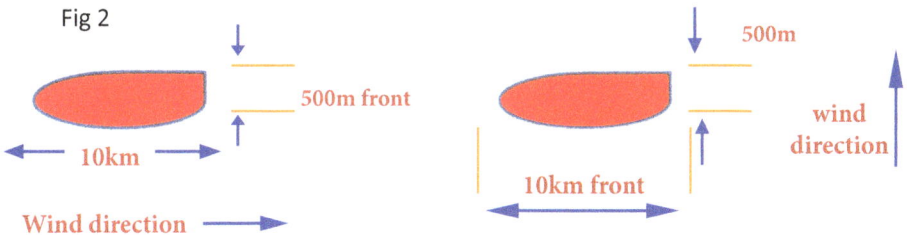

So now, you have a much wider threat and probably a powerful wind to push it forward.

REMEMBER:

To advise of fire, call 000

Ask for FIRE

State: Victoria

Where the fire is: Road/Street name,

Town name, Nearest crossroad.

House fire or bushfire.

Your name, address, phone number and map reference if possible.

The Black Saturday fire was in one sense unstoppable, because of the hot and extremely dry environment, combined with a strong wind moving the threat. The fire in some places jumped from ridge line, to ridge line, at a speed that didn't allow suppression.

In Victoria, the state is divided into districts. A district has its own geography and ways of accessibility. Each district is made up of regions, groups, and brigades. The Macedon Ranges shire is in the Central region. To give you an idea of the vastness of the Central region, it covers Daylesford in the north-west, down to Lorne in the south, then across to Wonthaggi, and up to Healesville in the east. This is a huge area in which the climate will vary from place to place, be it above the Great Dividing Range, or down nearer Bass Strait.

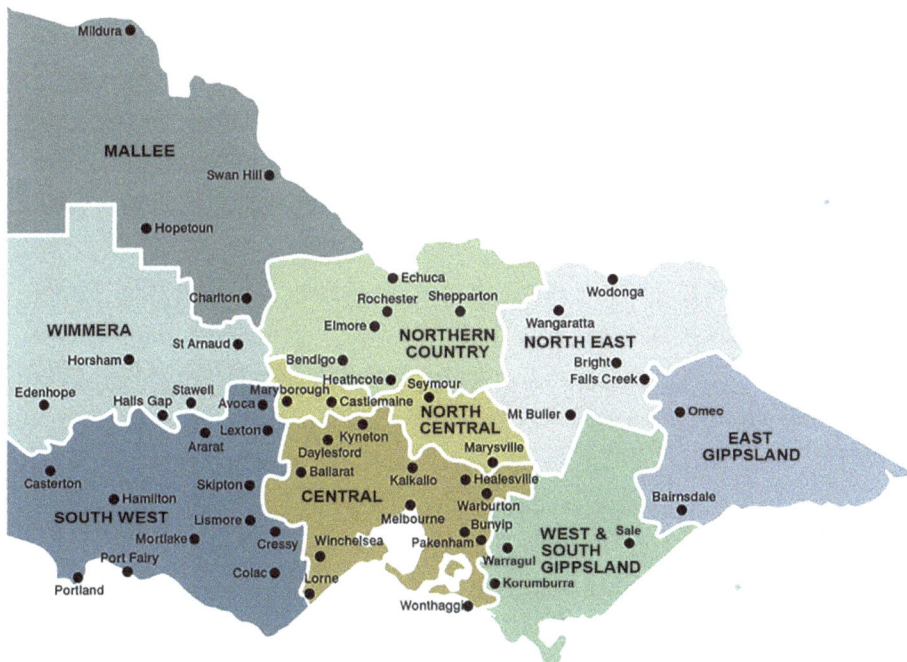

The fire districts of Victoria. The map can be found at CFA (www.cfa.vic.gov.au/warnings-restrictions/find-your-fire-district).

11

Warnings

"… long-range weather forecasts—no better than numbers
out of a hat." – Hugh McKay

How do you know if there is fire anywhere nearby? Will it be safe?
The question keeps occurring. If you are unsure of fire warnings,
environmental signs can help—what you can see, what you can hear,
what you can smell. Online, cfa.vic.gov.au. Listen to local radio. There
may or may not be fire sirens in your area, so do not necessarily expect
that warning.

Robert Manne writing of the evidence given at the Royal
Commission said, "… it had become clear that on 7 February both a
cumbersome bureaucratic structure and peculiar ideological mindset
had worked in combination to prevent the fire and emergency chiefs
… from issuing warnings to citizens…"[26]

It is important you remain alert, listen to local radio, and watch
for smoke.

The CFA recommends that if the warning is HIGH, EXTREME
or CATASTROPHIC, you should leave early, preferably the night
before. Advise friends and family of where you are going and how you
are travelling. If leaving just for the day, you might choose the local

26 Manne, Robert; *Making Trouble*, 2011, p153; also *The Monthly*, July 2009

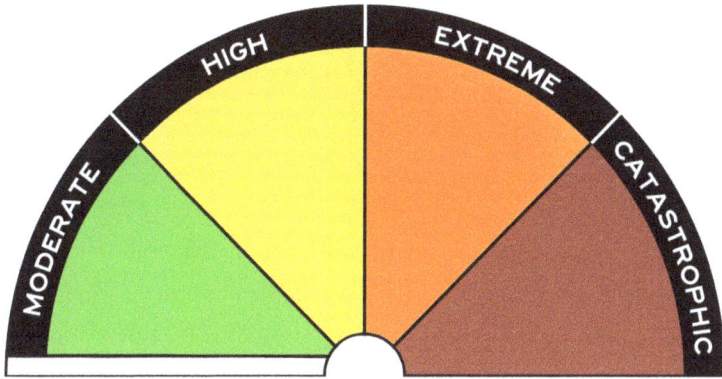

MODERATE	HIGH
Plan and prepare	Be ready to act

EXTREME	CATASTROPHIC
Take action now to protect life and property	For your survival, leave bushfire risk areas

cinema or shopping centre to enjoy the air conditioning. The question remains, will you be able to return home and when? And what if the fire starts at night and is not noticed until it is too late?

While the CFA is responsible under wildfire conditions, sometimes they stick too close to the 'rules'. In the book 'Making Trouble' Robert Manne tells us of the CFA Morwell Group Officer, Lou Sigmund. "In late January he saved many lives when he decided, against higher authority and settled policy, to sound the siren to evacuate his town. At every level, the professionals inside the CFA, and no doubt the DSE, were imprisoned by their organisations' mind-numbing bureaucratic rules. Conformity to rules was, in turn, the enemy of judgement, common sense and moral responsibility."[27]

Remember, it is recommended by the Country Fire Authority in Victoria to leave early. However, most people stay and wait to see what happens and then it may be too late. Once you have left home and if fire arrives, when can you return? That depends on what has happened. If the fire is within set boundaries or still within your area and not yet 'under control' you will not be allowed to return for reasons of safety or investigation.

The police on duty are unlikely to be locals. The local police will be involved in decision making like locating secure refuge areas or working and advising other authorities. The non-local police won't know you and will restrict entry under their instructions—nobody is to return until the 'all clear' is given.

Police will also be involved in dealing with people 'sight-seeing', some of whom plan to relieve you of things you have left behind—the lawn mower or other tools in the shed or, if the house remains or is little damaged, the TV or the jewellery left to you by your grandmother; the things that were important, but not worth collecting and filling the car with, perhaps your son's or daughter's favourite toy. Following Ash Wednesday Rodney Brown, upon returning to his Woodend farm, found that "… my troubles were not over. My fence posts were stolen, as was the gear box from my old Pontiac."[28]

Despite the warnings—be they right or wrong—if you are prepared, you are ready.

27 Manne, Robert; 2011 *Making Trouble*, p160
28 Rodney Brown in *Memories of Ash Wednesday*, 2023, p274

The country is inviting...

...and welcoming.

Above: Is there a house in there...? (There is.)

Below: A tangle of ladder fuels: leaf litter/twigs then low branches give fire an easy path upwards.

12

A late change of mind...
it may be too late

An important fact: In Victoria you cannot be required to evacuate.* Police and/or Fire Authority members may recommend you leave. Unlike New South Wales, evacuation is not compulsory. However, regulations may change.

In reference to fire prevention and preparedness, the 2003 Auditor General noted, "Residents who stay and actively defend their property also have a much better chance of survival than residents who leave at the last minute. Even in a vehicle, late evacuation is fraught with danger, exposing residents to extreme risk from radiant heat, a road crash in thick smoke, or hazards such as falling trees or power lines."[29]

When faced with real danger many of us forget the rules and behave erratically. During the Ash Wednesday fire there was a dangerous occasion where, "…we came to a bend in the road and found two cars travelling in the opposite direction, one tried to pass the other and so forced me off the road."[30] Fortunately, despite the damage, the family survived.

If you decide to leave early, where will you go? The city? The next town? To your cousin in Ocean Grove? You must consider—is it safe

*At time of publication – November 2023.
29 Cameron J.W.; 2003, *Fire prevention and preparedness,* p78
30 Harry Rutherford in *Memories of Ash Wednesday,* p246

there? Is there any accommodation? If so, is there a room and can I afford it? How long do we need to stay? Then of course, what will we take? Now there is a real question! Watching Craig Reucassel on the ABC 2020 program 'Big Weather', we heard homeowners' responses to a series of questions when he door knocked.

Reucassel asked, do you have a bushfire plan? The answer was 'No'.

What will you take with you?

— Chooks, bike, computer ...

Then, in a 10-minute trial, he asked them to collect whatever they thought important and leave in 10 minutes. What an interesting scenario ... all sorts of problems.

People expected fire fighters would be at 'their' home.

Next, where would you stop if driving and fire came?

What must you take with you to help with what may come next?

Because you are leaving, remember your medicines and prescriptions and whatever else you seriously need. If not kept in a fireproof safe at home, important documents must be taken with you. These should already be packed as part of pre-season planning. Take some snacks, money and special toys or things left to you over time. Next the laptop, or mini pad and anything else important. I can't decide for you, but you can't take everything.

The most important things apart from the personal goods are blankets and dust masks. They are to be used if you are trapped by fire when driving. Blankets must be made of wool or heavy cotton and **not synthetics** (they melt).

Having decided to leave because fire is in the area, what will you do if you encounter it? Driving can be very dangerous. If you are caught in a smoky situation, turn on all lights, including hazards.

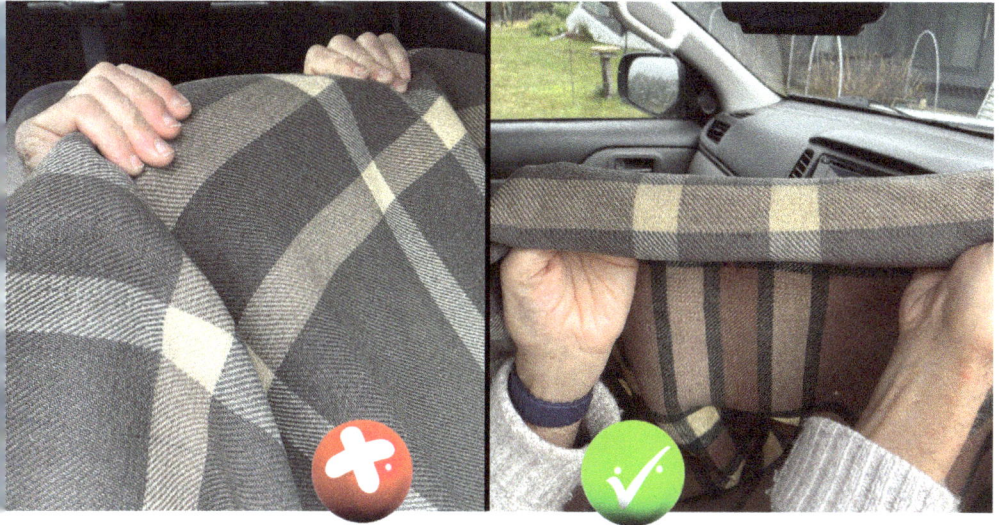

Do not leave hands exposed. Fold blanket over so hands are
hidden before pulling it up and over yourself...

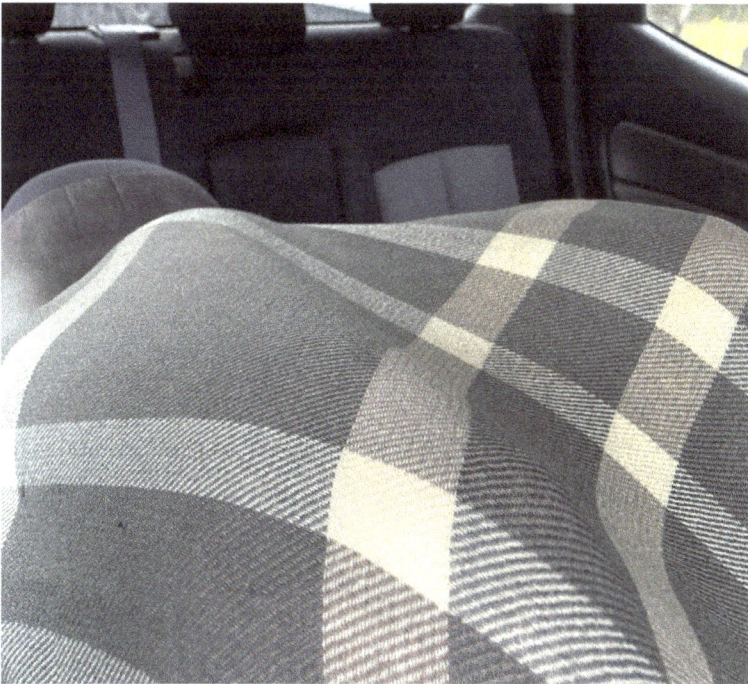

...and cover yourself totally.

If trapped, find a place as clear as possible from growth and scrub. Point the car towards the fire, giving you extra distance from the heat. Leave the engine running, close all vents and turn off any devices like the air conditioner or fan. Close the windows and get down as low as possible. Take a blanket each (or anything else suitable at hand) and fold it over so your hands are hidden, before pulling it up and over yourself. If there are children with you and depending on their age, put them under the blanket with you. Otherwise, make sure they are well covered. The fire will be intense but should pass by quickly. Do not leave the car, trying to outrun the heat. It won't work. Several people left their cars and died running from a fire at Lara, near Geelong, in the early 1970s.

Once the fire has passed the driver might check to see if all is safe. If the vehicle is ok, good. Otherwise wrap the blanket around you and get out onto the burnt ground and wait until someone comes by. This is not an easy thing to do, but you must stay.

In his memoir, Kerry O'Brien wrote, "Lisa Whitehead found another community in deep shock in the area around Wandong: Anne Coen, Hazeldene resident: 'We had to sit in the car and watch it coming over the hill. It was behind us and on both sides, and around the bend. It was coming in four directions'."[31]

Once home, what will you encounter? It is difficult to say. Where did the fire travel? Did it cross your property or pass by 200 metres away? Is your house still standing? If yes, what condition is it in—good, slightly damaged or, destroyed? If it has been destroyed, you have decisions to make—where will you go and who will support you? Local agencies via your council will be most likely.

If all is well with your house, what has happened to your neighbours? Are they there? Did their home survive? What is the overall

31 O'Brien, Kerry; 2018, p714

damage situation? Questions, questions, and yet more questions. Why didn't the Fire Brigade attend? The CFA has around 2000 fire trucks and while that is a lot of trucks, they cannot get to every property. Stopping the main fire is their priority. Remember, they are there to stop the main fire; assisting property owners is secondary.

13

Equipment

Yes, even a water pistol

Sprinklers are a really good idea, though to have them installed will not be cheap. However, they can also be used to water the surrounding garden during the year; but remember to keep your tank full coming up to summer. Keep in mind that you cannot rely on mains water during a bushfire, meaning you will need a pump to maintain water supply to your system. Now, where do you install them? How powerful should they be and what is the best way to bring water to them?

A **tank** that can supply water for use in the home and the garden, as well as for fire protection, will be a real investment. The cost of a large tank, depending on capacity, will vary and you are best to seek advice. I have a metal 95,000-litre model because we are not on town water. I suggest a tank able to hold 30,000 litres would be adequate, but I would recommend having someone advise you. If you are on mains water, can you be sure the supply will not be interrupted due to loss of power, usage by those around you or further away? That is another good reason to build your own supply. On top of this, as noted earlier you must have a reliable and independent pumping system. This should be run on petrol or diesel. You cannot rely on the electrical supply to be constant, due to falling trees or fire.

Some simple but invaluable equipment: Mop, spade, rake, bucket for water and a pressure water pistol.

Next, getting water to the sprinklers. This will require a plumber or other tradesperson to install or advise just how to go about the installation. The pipes must be buried, or at least well hidden from heat and fire. Metal is best and while some other products available are very good, they may melt. As far as sprinklers go, they should be set to rain on the buildings.

Fire hoses. These are available from most country farm supply businesses and will cost around $200 to $400. They must be fitted properly and situated where they can be useful in protecting the home. Please remember, if you buy a cheap fire hose, you get a hose that may not last the years of your time at your property. As far as training to use such equipment goes, your volunteer brigade should be able to assist.

If you are reliant on electricity, a **generator** is next on your shopping list. The reason is if the power goes out you will be stranded. Prices vary and depend on your real needs.

14

Preparation

"… and we had been caught unprepared" – Frances Wearne[32]

People living in bushfire prone areas will need to prepare their properties each year in readiness for the fire season. Fire areas include suburban homes close to forests and open grasslands. A family fire plan should be in place and may need regular updating. On Total Fire Ban days, more intense preparation needs to occur. At this point, decisions need to be made about leaving early or staying to defend if fire should occur. The highest level of preparation comes when bushfire threatens.

Fires can take place at any time. It does not have to be a hot summer's day. The day can be warm, say 25 degrees, with a light wind blowing. If the fuels are dry and somehow a spark lands amongst them, we might have a fire. While the conditions may seem low, a nasty blaze can get up and running. That is why we say, **be prepared**.

If we remove the fuels and create space between fuel and buildings, we have gone a long way in getting ready for fire.

Clearing is the first job, which continues for the rest of the year and begins again next year. Remove all plants and wooden structures within 5 to 10 metres of the building. This removes materials that can burn in the dry conditions, or lead to the starting of a fire on an

32 Frances Wearne in *Memories of Ash Wednesday*, 2023, p159

adjacent property. The main thing is to maintain this safe distance throughout the year. If you begin today and continue for 12 months, you will achieve a greater safety zone. If possible, clear a metre next to the house and put a layer of gravel around the house. This is a way of stopping any ignition close to the house.

The Age newspaper in Melbourne published in 2019 a picture of an American home headed 'Paradise saved'. The text read, "Sean and Dawn Herr … with their house, survived the devastating Camp fire in Paradise, California, last November. The Herrs adhered to strict building codes, including encircling their 2010 home in gravel to keep flames back."[33]

Next, although you may not feel safe at heights, for tasks such as climbing on to the roof or removing leaves from the gutters, have someone remove any overhanging trees or large branches. This helps prevent falling limbs breaking tiles or windows, allowing entry of embers. Then there are the gutters around the roof. These are a real danger if filled with leaves and other combustibles. The best idea is to have gutter guard fitted to help prevent a build-up of dangerous materials. If your home is on stumps, metal flywire can be used to guard against embers going under the building.The important things to remove are the small twigs and leaves. These are the main contributors to a fire getting started. Small items dry quickly, heat quickly and burn easily. Although large logs and branches are not the real concern, it is a good idea to remove the smaller branches.

As far as the green grass surrounding your home goes, how long should it be? There are several opinions about this. If the grass is more than 50mm (2 inches) then in the event of fire, the dry air and heat will cause a hotter fire. The longer the grass, the worse the fire will be. However, green grass about 50mm high will, hopefully, stop

33 *The Age,* 11 April 2019, p15

A border of gravel surrounding your home will help stop
ignition close to the house.

those invading embers catching, allowing you to put water on them. Keeping garden areas cool by applying water during high fire danger weather is a way to stop fire should it approach. If you are reliant on tank water, think before you water: you may need it in the summer.

Check if you have any openings around the house, for example, gaps between facia boards where embers may get in. These can be protected by covering in metal fly wire.

David Bowman said, "Many people ... have chosen to reside in naturally flammable landscapes to enjoy the amenity of living in forests away from the concrete and stress of cities. What is often overlooked ... is that the beautiful green sylvan retreats have naturally and periodically erupted into deadly fire storms."[34]

Mountain retreats are beautiful: but go into this lifestyle with eyes wide open, and be prepared.

34 Bowman D; 2011

Preparation is a never-ending job, so if you do a little each week you will have an easier workload. The fire pump is another thing needing attention. If you wish it to work when required, you must check it at least once a month. That means starting it and making sure the hose connected is in order. It is no good if you encounter trouble starting it when the fire is heading in your direction. So, if you start it each month or week, run it for 5 minutes. At the beginning of summer, do a full check. You will be more secure. An important thing about petrol-powered pumps is the fuel used. If you have not started the pump for a few months, the fuel may be stale and must be removed. Put fresh petrol in the tank.

You can purchase a fireproof safe for $300 to $500 to protect those extra special jewels and watches, along with copies of documents like your insurance, bank details and wills. It is important to remember that if you open your safe too soon after fire, the contents may explode in flame because of the built-up internal heat. WAIT.

Make a fire plan. Families need to have a plan which covers tasks to be carried out and of course, arrangements to cover the stay or leave decision. Suggestions and a checklist for what to include appears at the end of this publication. It is a good idea to review and practise this plan each year.

Put together a clothes box. If you should find yourself threatened by fire it is recommended to have suitable clothing in the one spot ready to put on. What to include is covered in detail in the Clothing chapter.

On a Total Fire Ban day there is work to be done. Check the fire rating—particularly High, Extreme, or more importantly a Catastrophic day. Have a fire plan ready to enact. Be aware that a bushfire can occur on any day. It does not have to be a Total Fire Ban day. The higher the fire danger rating, the higher the risk. Catastrophic is the highest and the most dangerous.

WHEN PREPARING

Remove all plants within 5 metres of house. Particularly those near windows.

Remove tree branches overhanging the house.

Remove leaves and grasses which may have started growing in the gutter. Install gutter guard.

Remove firewood stacked near buildings.

Remove shrubs under trees along with leaves and grasses.

Remove any 'triangle' which may promote burning.

Remove anything close to driveway.

On a day where there is a likelihood of fire, check the list of tasks to be done and assign them to the appropriate family member. Pull mats away from doorways and any nearby furniture. Sweep up leaf litter from around the house, particularly if you have a veranda. Run the fire pump and have garden hoses ready. Collect mops, rakes, brooms, buckets, and wheelie bins and have them at the ready. It is a good idea to block your downpipes using tennis balls or plugs from the garden store. Next, fill the gutters with water. Most important, if you have bottled gas, make sure the relief valve is pointed away from any structure.

All the time be aware of what you might hear – sirens; smell – smoke; see – smoke.

If it is your plan to stay and defend, or it is too late to leave, what are the neighbours doing? Staying or going? If they are planning to stay, talk to them about what they are doing and whether you can work together. If they are leaving, where do they plan to go and how can you contact them. This information can be helpful once the fire has passed. Psychologists say that feeling you are not alone increases the feeling of wellbeing, raising your confidence.

Living in paradise is something to which we all aspire. Preparation is more than physical; it includes knowing the risks of your geography and how the emergency systems work. During the Ash Wednesday fire, a CFA member received calls in which, "People screamed down the phone at me 'Where are the tankers? What will I do? Where will I go? Help me damn you! And once or twice, some less polite words were used."[35]

One home survived because of careful preparation: "I decided to fill up all the containers … the rubbish bins, the blue barrel and connected all the tap hoses and checked the flow … we both wet all the wooden parts of the house."[36]

35 Kenworthy, Morna; 2007, *Aftermath of fire : a people's triumph,* p14
36 Rhonda Irving in *Memories of Ash Wednesday,* (Power ed.) 2023, p174

Mt Disappointment Road, Whittlesea, Black Saturday 2009.
Photo Heather Knight

15

Clothing
Those old overalls and leather garden gloves etc

In the event of a fire in or near your property, it is important to cover up. Clothing MUST be of loose-fitting natural materials. In a fire, synthetic fabrics will attach to your skin and be most unpleasant or even life-changing. No shorts, T shirts or thongs! You should be fully covered by a long-sleeved shirt and lightweight long pants. A damp cloth around the neck will help stop hot ash warming your body. Leather gloves and a full-brimmed hat that can be securely attached are needed, along with goggles for the eyes. If you haven't got a pair, they are cheap at hardware stores. Although uncomfortable in hot conditions, a dust mask will be a great help in avoiding smoke inhalation. Footwear is vital. No thongs or sandals—only boots or thick-soled leather shoes. Boots are best because of their overall support and strength.

It is most important to cover as much of your body as possible. Coverage reduces the heat you are exposed to and if you maintain fluid intake, you should be ok. Shorts and singlets may seem to be a good idea for keeping cool, but no. The stinging of embers can be rotten! Or worse. Now that you are ready, remember the children. Their clothing should be the same type as yours.

Burns are horrific. If you or another are caught under a hail of embers, the best way to treat burns is water. Just pour cold water gently over to remove the heat. If it should be worse, apply wet towels and or continue allowing water to wash over the burns. Call an ambulance and while this may not arrive, you must try.

In the event of a fire bomber flying over while you are outside, it is probably best to move inside or under a veranda, to avoid injury. <u>Do not shelter under a tree</u>.

RECOMMENDED TYPE OF CLOTHING

16

A concrete shelter?
Perhaps a personal bunker

Geoff Hudson, speaking on the ABC's *Ockham's Razor* program in 2010, said, "Where are the underground shelters to protect the people? May I suggest there is a simple answer: Mass-produced fire shelters."

While this is not a new idea, it is worth considering.

Depending on where you live, the local environment and topography will play an important part in deciding whether it is worthwhile to install a concrete shelter and how it should be built. If you do decide to invest $8000 to $15,000 in a bunker, how can you ensure its suitability? Is it smoke-proof? Is it truly resistant to direct flame attack? How long could you remain inside safely? If large enough, could it be a place where you could temporarily live while a new home is being constructed, should your house be destroyed by fire?

If the fire bunker is not utilised over the years, do not fall into the trap of using it as a storage facility. When needed, it may be impossible to access.

If you decide to go ahead with such a shelter, think about its use both during a fire, and afterwards. Will it have power, water, a bed or other home-type facilities? ...something to think about. On the other hand, if you are rebuilding and are thinking of the future, a bunker could be an important part of the new design.

If you are thinking of building a bunker, have a look at www. cfa.vic.gov.au/plan-prepare/private-bushfire-shelters-or-bunkers, or check a story in *The Sydney Morning Herald* of 16 February 2009 by Daniel Lewis headed, "Cellars and dugouts could become death traps".

17

Burning off, pets, holidays etc
Some things not to be forgotten

Burning off is something many of us take for granted. Yeah, she'll be right mate. But it is important to check local regulations before lighting up, with either the CFA or local council. Register your burn with Emergency Services. Tell your neighbours what you are doing and check the weather forecast to make sure the burn will be safe. Make sure the area surrounding your burn is clear of any flammable materials. You can water the surrounding area prior to burning. Importantly, make sure you have someone with you or watching what is happening. Then when the burn is over, extinguish any burning or smouldering materials. To allow them to keep burning is a risk.

Pets

Then there are your pets. Think about them on high-risk days; where and how they will be kept. During the Ash Wednesday fire, some of those people driving over Mt Macedon were, I was told, leading horses to safety, and slowing the traffic flow. And so, it is most important to be well prepared and thoughtful of others evacuating, along with avoiding other dangers.

Holidays

Then there is holiday time. Where are you going this summer? Is the caravan park open? Will it remain open if there is a fire in the area? Where will you be able to go if there is a fire? Have you told your friends and neighbours where you are going? Do they know how to contact you in the event of fire or other important event? Importantly, do not travel through areas where fire is burning. Don't forget, you can talk to your Fire Brigade before the fire season or visit the CFA website cfa.vic.gov.au.

18

The First Australians
65,000 years of history

The First Australians are the original inhabitants of this country. They lived with the land, unlike the arrivals of later years, who live from the land. First Nations populations used fire as a source of management when working land, herding native animals and sourcing food, in an efficient way. In comparison, modern Australia seems to use everything in our power to make money and then complains when fire tears our dreams apart.

"...large fires were apparently extremely rare before European occupation; the movement of Europeans into the area brought a massive increase in both the frequency and intensity of fires," fire researcher Jenny Indian wrote in a 2008 CSIRO publication.[37]

In his book *The Biggest Estate on Earth*, Bill Gammage wrote of how the first inhabitants kept the land, quoting farmer/squatter Anne Drysdale commenting in 1841 on a river near Geelong: "This place is really beautiful. A short distance from the Barwon, a noble river: all so green and fresh with the trees of the finest kinds ... scattered about, and in clumps, like a Nobleman's Park."[38]

I have worked with members of our Indigenous community and asked many questions about their way of living. The children learn the ways of the older members of the community as they grow. This happens through experience and taking part in helping the older people. When

37 Indian, Jenny, 2008, *Community Bushfire Safety*, CSIRO, p37
38 Gammage, Bill, 2011, *The Biggest Estate on Earth*, p95

working with a community 200 kilometres west of Alice Springs, we were interested in how the people found food. While walking in the outback we asked, where do you find bush honey? Along the way, a child reached up into a bush and picked something resembling a piece of cotton wool. When I tasted it, it was not like the honey we are used to, hardly sweet at all. Later, crossing the Fink River bed, we were shown how to find yams and within minutes, our palms were filled. How does this apply to fire? It relates to being aware of your surroundings—how the wind blows; the way the trees direct the wind; how far you can see if you are watching for smoke or other signs of fire.

Resolving the problem of fire might be as simple as watching the weather. Kaurna elder Lewis Yarlupurka O'Brien tells the story of walking with Aunty May. "She said, 'Lewis, you see that bird on the tree at the corner?' .... But she wasn't really asking me if I saw the bird. She actually wanted to know if I was watching, and observing, and listening to what was going on around me."[39]

To survive, must we become more aware of our place in this country?

On a trip to the Grampians once, I asked a local when did they carry out a burn? The answer came, in July when the wattle trees begin flowering, because that is when the damp slows fire and only the dry things burn. Burning has been a part of the First Nations' way. Archaeologist Josephine Flood writes of how the early settlers found places not unlike parts of the UK—open park-like country, caused by the regular effect of burning every 3 or 4 years to maintain an open land. When the Aboriginal people were moved away, the scrub returned, obliterating the land used for grazing. If we note the way in which the traditional owners managed the land and follow their example, we might not have the bushfire problems we currently have.

39 O'Brien, Lewis Yarlupurka; 2007, *And The Clock Struck Thirteen*, p99

By burning 'lightly', now known as 'cool burns' the First Nations people did not destroy the environment. They helped it to grow and maintain itself. For thousands of years, fire-stick farming reduced the risk of uncontrolled burning. Flood describes how the Indigenous used fire. By burning the dead grass and leaves, they encouraged new growth. New growth invited the local animals to return and, in that way, provided the people with access to food. "Aborigines used fire not only for cooking, but also as a hunting weapon, igniting the bush both to drive out game and to make fresh new grass to spring up to attract browsing animals."[40]

In his book *Dark Emu*, Bruce Pascoe noted, "The importance of fire was evidenced by the fact that after the fires of 'Ash Wednesday' 1983, there was phenomenal flowering of tuberous perennials. These had adapted to the horticultural intercession of man and fire and become a crucial part of plant ecology."[41]

Victor Steffensen wrote of how the Indigenous burnt and how it protected the environment; "The fire starts off slowly, letting out the smell of smoke so that everything will know it is coming. Giving all the animals time to respond to the fire and move to safer areas. Because we don't burn all the country at once, the animals do not have to go far to get to safe ground. … Tiny little insects … crawled out of the grass and up the trees for safety. They know that being in the trees means they are safe, since the right fire will hardly leave a fire scar on the tree trunks. … All those insects escaping the fire, thousands of lives saved instantly that are important to the lifecycles are food sources to larger animals."[42]

If we continue allowing 'rubbish' to accumulate, we are providing amounts of kindling, which in turn helps create devastating fires. If we want to live safely, we should consider returning to the ways of those who lived in this country before Europeans arrived.

40 Flood, Josephine; 2004, *Archaeology of the Dreamtime,* p115
41 Pascoe, Bruce; 2014, *Dark Emu,* p120
42 Steffensen, V.; 2020, *Fire Country,* p155-56

19

At the end of the day
Is it just a house, or your home?

To rebuild following fire can be more expensive because of changes to building regulations. For example, certain materials may not be allowed, entry points for embers will need to be considered and the building redesigned. Double glazing may be compulsory and who can guess what else? Along with that, is the amount you were insured for enough to rebuild as you would wish? If you are about to build a new home or renovate an existing one, now is the time to consider such ideas. The installation of a water tank and watering system can be done more easily and more cheaply if done at the same time as the house construction.

As for staying or leaving, remember all you have learnt and think carefully about the way in which you will react in the face of a major fire. Will you stay each time you are threatened, or will you leave? Will you leave early every time fire codes are above Very High and return to find nothing has happened and so, remain at home for the next, and the next? Or will you move into a suburban area, prepared to miss life in the 'bush'?

Raising your awareness and sharing your concerns about bushfire with friends and neighbours will allow them the opportunity to share their thoughts and ideas of how they might react in the event of a major threat. It might allow you to work more as a community aiding each other with preparation and workload.

These ideas are to help you in times of threat so that the house, the family and pets, should be safe. When fire has burnt the scrub, leaving a blackened earth, hopefully within a few months in this a part of the landscape you will see the regeneration of the land and discover plants you did not know were part of the country.

From 1770, with the arrival of the English, to today, along with global warming we must adapt to the land and the way it is changing.

Picture Heather Knight

Regrowth after Black Saturday fires 1: Belladonna lilies.

"Prehistoric Aboriginal society was dynamic. Neither the land nor the people were unchanging, and it is the constant human adaptation to a changing environment that provides both the challenge and fascination of Australian prehistory."[43]

The First Australians, "They sanctioned key principles: think long term; leave the world as it is; think globally, act locally; ally with fire; control population. They were active, not passive, striving for balance and continuity to make all life abundant, convenient and predictable."[44]

Should we mirror the old ways and maintain a safer place?

Picture Heather Knight

Regrowth after Black Saturday fires 2: Mt Disappointment.

43 Flood, Josephine, 2004, *Archaeology of the Dreamtime*, p280
44 Gammage, Bill; 2011, *The Biggest Estate on Earth*, p323

CHECKLIST

- make a Fire Plan and practise it
- check whether your gate is wide enough for a fire truck to enter
- gate kept opened or closed?
- create a mini fire break between your driveway and your home
- install a sprinkler system attached to an independent water supply
- have a water tank and keep it nearly full
- have a petrol or diesel-powered pump
- store additional fuel for pump in a safe place
- have a fire hose that will reach the areas around the house
- check the pump and fire hose regularly to see they are working
- have garden hoses that can be used to wet down areas around the house
- clean the gutters and consider installing gutter mesh
- cover gaps and spaces to prevent entry of embers
- clear vegetation 10 to 15 metres or more from the house, including kindling
- have mops, buckets, wheelie bins, pump water pistol, ladder/s, ready and accessible
- keep supply of bottles of water

- **store a box of correct clothing for all family members**
- **keep personal safety items at hand — goggles, mask, wet cloth for neck**
- **check if home and contents insurance is up to date**
- **store documents in a fireproof safe or keep packed together ready to be taken**
- **know which medications will need to be taken with you should you leave**
- **know which treasured items you will be taking should you leave**
- **have a battery powered radio to hear news**
- **have a cage to transport pets**
- **consider which vehicle/s you will use should you need to leave early**
- **find out if there are any dedicated refuge areas in your area**
- **familiarise yourself with possible road escape routes**
- **have a list of neighbour's phone numbers**
- **use local fire brigade to give you pre-season information**

Remember, everything you can have ready beforehand will help to make you fire ready and add to your security should bushfire threaten.

FIRE PLAN
Make sure all family members are familiar with the Fire Plan
and have practised it.

Plan to leave early on Total Fire Ban days   Yes   No

We will drive to [accommodation or family/friends]

. . . .

Our emergency route will be . . . .

 or . . . .

Family members who will travel with us. . . . .

. . . .

We have a disabled family member to be catered for . . . .

We plan to take our pets with us   Yes   No

Method of transport. . . . .

Arrangement for livestock. . . . .

People we will tell if leaving early. . . . .

Number of woollen blankets to put in car. . . . .

First aid kit up to date and ready. . . . .

Driver's licence and mobile phone. . . . .

Important phone numbers:

Family. . . . .

friends . . . .

neighbours........................... doctor......................

Important documents to store in a fireproof safe or take with us:

. . . .

List of valuables we will take with us ....

. . . .

List of toys we will take with us......................................

List of medication/prescriptions we will take with us...............

. . . .

List of toiletries we will take with us................................

Drinks, snacks, food items to take with us ....

. . . .

Pet food..

We plan to stay and defend   Yes   No

Location of survival clothing and protective equipment.............

. . . .

Family members who will stay.....................................

List of jobs for each person staying to defend......................

. . . .

Person to drive the car if part of the family leaves..................

These are examples of items to go on a Fire Plan. Add items which are important or relevant to your situation. Keep in mind that if the choice is to stay and defend, it is optimal to have more than one person.

20

Recollections

The following are the recollections of three volunteer fire fighters

Bruce Dudon:

On January 1st, 2006, a fire occurred near Lancefield, Central Victoria. During our work we were totally engulfed by smoke. We weren't under threat of fire, simply unable to see where we could move safely. As the driver, I turned on all lights including the flashing red and blue, closed the windows and waited until we could see a way out. Fortunately, the wind changed, and we were able to return to work.

It is difficult to see clearly during a fire.

John H:

"*I was part of a strike team on New Year's Day attending a fire near Lancefield. After some blacking work, we were assigned to help put out some burning hay. Soon our role became that of ferrying water to the appliances with fixed monitors. After several uneventful trips, on nearing the hay fire, with no warning at all, we found ourselves in a dense cloud of smoke and soot. There was no visibility, and breathing was difficult. Neither of us on the back of the truck had our breathing masks handy as we simply did not expect to be needing them—and had been preoccupied with the task of filling and emptying our water tank. We sat as still as possible to reduce the need for air while breathing as slowly as possible through cloth. Because of this lack of activity, we were ok, although we did urge the driver to get a move on. Remaining where we were in the midst of thick smoke was not conducive to our health, whatever the reason confronting the drivers.*

"*Eventually, we moved, the smoke dissipated, and none the worse for the experience apart from a very sooty appearance, we got back to pumping the water into the fire-fighting tanker.*"

Ian L:

"I have not experienced anything quite like it before, but I imagine that it is quite like being suddenly dropped into deep water before you have had time to take a breath.

"Last year I was a crewman on a fire truck at a bush fire near Baynton in northwest Victoria. We were tasked with the boring but necessary task of trying to put out a large stack of round hay bales— difficult at the best of times but in this instance made more so because of the high temperatures, a strong northerly wind and the fact that hay bales are very compact and there were a lot of them.

"We had been pouring literally thousands of litres of water onto the stack and had just been down to the assembly point to fill our tank and were returning for another assault. As we were approaching the stack, the wind changed, and the truck was enveloped in a combination of smoke, steam and embers.

"Because of the density of the smoke, the driver of the truck was forced to stop for fear of running into something. You may not be aware that the crewmen on the truck ride in the back in the open air and as the truck had stopped, within seconds we were enveloped in dense smoke with a complete inability to breathe clean air.

"Like being immersed in water, panic was the first emotion, a complete sense of being lost, unable to see anything and unable to breath. However, training takes over and as we have access to face masks, after a moment or two we were able to slip them on and breath relatively normally.

"Slightly scary, but we were soon out of it and able to resume our tasks. However, a lesson learned and now I make sure that I and my fellow crewmen carry a mask at all times in bush fire conditions—you just never know."

Bairnsdale at what time of day? ...2pm.

The fire truck approaches a blaze at Colo Heights, Sydney, in 2001.
Picture by Peter Nightscales, volunteer fire fighter, Mt Macedon Brigade.

A closer look at the roof shows how the old stable is loaded with dry pine needles, a robust fuel.

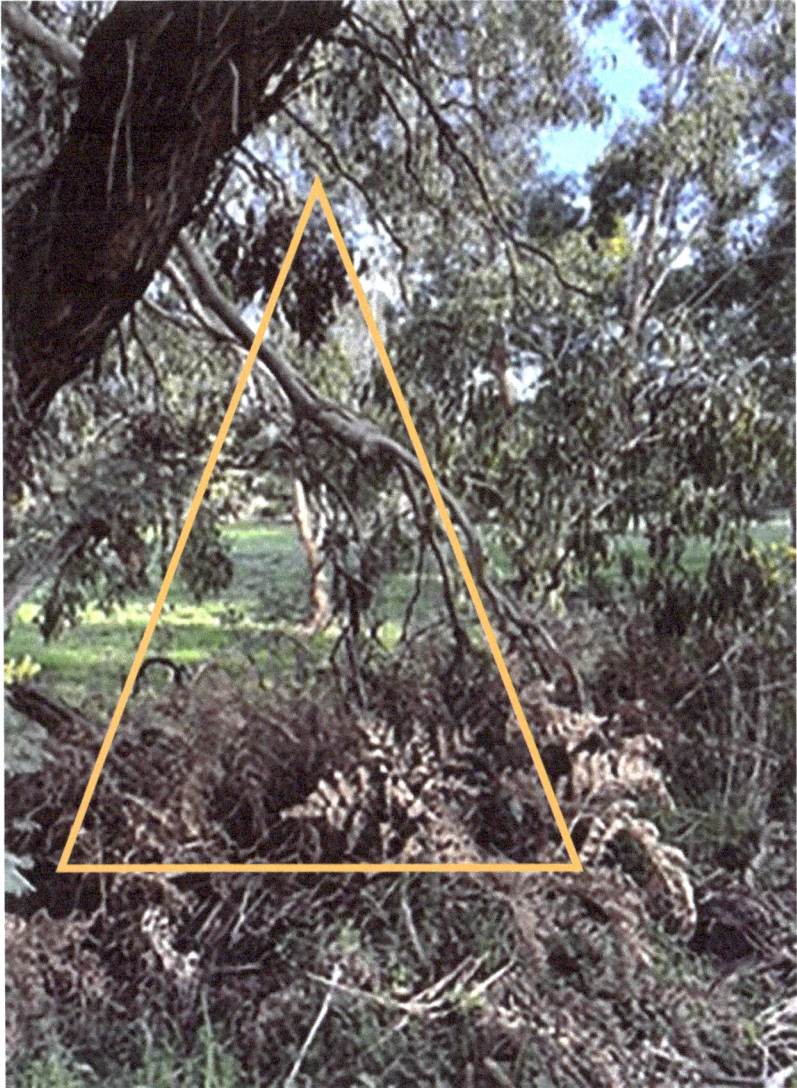

Another example of the fuel ladder: Low dry brush and low-hanging branches lead fire upwards.

21

Comments

No one knows what will actually happen when a bushfire occurs. I have included some comments regarding the prediction and outcomes of tragic events.

Hugh Mackay has made comments re 'The positive outcomes of good intentions.'

"... long range weather forecasts—one month ahead—were no better than numbers pulled out of a hat. So impatient are we to know what will happen next, we are in danger of losing sight of our ability to shape our own futures. The commentator who is prepared to predict an election result seems more interesting, and certainly more 'expert', than the one who suggests we should focus on what's at stake, then wait until people have voted so we can see who has actually won."

Professor Mark Creamer of Melbourne University on 'The mental health effects of traumatic experience': "We've come a long way in our understanding of mental health response to trauma ... but many challenges lie ahead. ... I suspect we will never prevent it completely, but we can minimise it by good preparation, early recognition and effective management of problems when they arise. In a similar vein, how should we respond with whole communities following widespread disaster such as bushfires, flood or earthquakes?"

In a letter to *The Age*, Melbourne, headed 'Taking responsibility for where you live', National Recovery and Resilience Agency coordinator Shane Stone asks why people would want to live 'among the gum trees' following disastrous floods. This recalls Victoria's then planning minister Matthew Guy's jibe after floods in 2012: "If Labor and the Greens and their associates have such concerns about bushfire risk in the Green Wedge, why then do the people making these claims still live there?" – *The Age*, 10 September 2012.

There are many reasons why people live in such areas: some have been there for generations, others have taken advantage of more affordable housing, while others want to move away from an ever-increasing urbanisation. However, residents need to act in advance to mitigate risk. This involves formulating an emergency plan to leave early, preparing a property appropriately, having a back-up plan or two (maybe a personal bunker) and so on.

It is not an easy task. Gender dysfunction emerged as a key issue in a local survey following a bushfire—ie, he wants to stay, she wants to go. Also, after time, memories of disasters fade and complacency returns. New residents often have no idea about what might happen. Volunteer and emergency services work with the community to ensure awareness and compliance. Nevertheless, it is an uphill struggle. Responsibility and awareness, first and foremost, lies with residents. – Dick Davies, North Warrandyte, *The Age* 11 March 2022.

In 2017 Professor Jim McLennan et al from La Trobe University presented a review paper titled *Should We Leave Now? Behavioural Factors in Evacuation Under Wildfire Threat*. Within it is an examination of 'Possible Actions by Authorities to Address Late Wildfire Evacuations [Item 5.3],' as follows:
"There are several actions that can be taken by authorities to reduce

the number of residents who will delay evacuating following wildfire warnings.

1. Continue to improve the accuracy, comprehensiveness, timeliness, and location specificity of wildfire warnings for residents in at-risk locations so as to reduce householder uncertainty about their threat situation and thus encourage early survival decisions and actions. Ongoing developments in social media-based communications and technology are likely to contribute and new applications need to be developed and trialled.

2. Increase householders' knowledge and understanding of the risks involved in last-minute flight or last-ditch defence of an underprepared property.

3. Reduce householders' reluctance to leave by:

[a] assisting them with advice about preparations to leave which are minimally inconvenient but sufficient to survive, encouraging planning for staged moves to successively safer locations during the course of a wildfire event as their known threat level increases, and providing pre-fire information about likely safe evacuation destinations and routes. [b] emphasising that a house can be prepared to survive, wildfire attack without the resident having to be present to actively defend it. 'The safest place to be during a wildfire is somewhere else, and here are things to do so that your house is more likely be standing when you return'.

[c] concentrating on advising householders about low-cost actions they can take to reduce vulnerability to bushfire, such as clearing vegetation and combustibles from around the house, rather than emphasising more costly measures such as retro-fitting the house with fire-resistant construction materials.

[d] emphasising the importance of being prepared to leave before a fire is near and providing clear and simple advice on what such preparation entails.

[e] allaying concerns about looting.

[f] emphasising that while residents should be alert for wildfire warnings from authorities, they should not expect to be contacted individually and told when to leave; they should instead decide beforehand on their own 'triggers' for leaving safely prior to imminent threat, and actively monitor the emerging fire situation utilising both the media information and environmental cues."

By way of a concluding comment, the last point [f] seems likely to present a particular challenge for fire agencies: how best to help residents understand what, for their situation, is likely to constitute an 'imminent' wildfire threat necessitating immediate evacuation? This issue clearly needs further research.

This paralysis of indecision can lead to people leaving late when conditions are the most dangerous, or not being able to get out at all.

According to research, people with experience are more likely to leave, and those who are more vulnerable make plans to evacuate early. "They're particularly likely to make that decision if they have young children, if they're elderly and just accept that there's no way they're up to defending the property," Dr McLennan said. That extended to people who may have a disability.

According to the CFA, defending a property requires at least two able-bodied, fit and determined adults who understand that the process of fending off a bushfire can take hours, and sometimes even days, of extreme effort.

Dr McLennan, who has spent time in the field with CFA volunteers, said people who had never experienced a bushfire were likely to underestimate the effort required to defend a property from one.

"For most of us we see bushfires; we see them on television happening somewhere else to someone else," he said. "It takes away the sheer awfulness of it."

He said people who had encountered a bushfire before were more likely to leave as they had a better understanding of how dangerous it could be.

There is also a third cohort according to Dr McLennan, a psychologist working with the Bushfire Cooperative Research Centre through La Trobe University.

Dr McLennan

"They're often older males who aren't going to be pushed around by anybody," he said. "Social psychologists have a term for this called 'psychological reactance'. It's a kind of pushback when you think you're being told what to do."

It was an irrational, but human response.

"I think most of us have had an experience of someone in authority trying to tell us how to live our lives, and we bristle at that," he said.

There was also a fairly well-established phenomenon of elderly people being far more reluctant to leave the home, something he discovered while researching the 2009 Black Saturday bushfires.

"[There were] a number of quite tragic cases of elderly people who were living alone, getting phone calls from sons and daughters begging them to leave and sort of saying, 'I'm not sure if I need to leave now' or 'I'll wait until a fire person comes and tells me it's time to leave'," he said. "There was a reluctance to actually take the decisive step before leaving."

Bibliography and books worth reading

Alexander, D., Gaillard, J.C. and Wisner, B., 2012, *Handbook of Hazards and Disaster Risk Reduction,* Routledge

Babugura, Agnes A.; 2012 *Children, youth and disaster,* Routledge

Bowman, David; 23 July 2011, 'Fire and humans', *Ockham's Razor,* ABC Radio National

Cameron, J.W.; 2003, *Fire prevention and preparedness,* Auditor-General Victoria, published by Government Printer, Melbourne, Victoria

Clode, Danielle; 2010, *A Future In Flames,* Melbourne University Press

Cormick, Craig; *Ockham's Razor,* ABC RN, 23 October 2011

Curnow, Karen; 2010, *The Flipside of Misfortune, A Journey Through Change in Challenging Times* (a personal story of Curnow's Black Saturday experiences) Bookpal

Flood, Josephine; 2004, *Archaeology of the Dreamtime,* JB Publishing

Gammage, Bill; 2011, *The Biggest Estate on Earth,* Allen & Unwin

Goodman, Helen and Proudley, Mae; 2008, *Community Bushfire Safety,* CSIRO Publishing

Hansen, Christine & Griffiths, Tom; 2012, *Living with fire,* CSIRO Publishing

Hudson, Geoff; 2010, *Ockham's Razor,* ABC RN www.abc.net.au/rn/0ckhamsrazor/2010/2803822.htm

Hyland, Adrian; 2011, *Kinglake-350,* Text Publishing Company

Indian, Jenny; 2008, *Community Bushfire Safety,* CSIRO Publishing

Kanowski, P., Whelan, R.J. & Ellis, S.; 2004, National inquiry on bushfire mitigation and management, Council of Australian Governments

Kenworthy, Morna; 2007, *Aftermath of fire : a people's triumph,* East Brunswick, Victoria

Knight, Heather, & Turnbull, Catherine (eds); 2015, *The Long Way Home – personal accounts of Black Saturday and the bushfire recovery in Mitchell Shire*. Publisher: Heather Knight and Catherine Turnbull. (Try Kilmore Library, Mitchell Shire, if not available locally.)

Manne, Robert; 2011, *Making Trouble,* Black Inc Agenda

O'Brien, Kerry; 2018, *Kerry O'Brien – A Memoir,* Allen & Unwin

O'Brien, Lewis Yarlupurka, AO; 2007, *And The Clock Struck Thirteen,* Wakefield Press

'Paradise saved', *The Age* 2019, The Age Company Pty Ltd

Pascoe, Bruce; 2014, *Dark Emu,* Magabala Books

Power, Bryan (ed.); 2023, *Memories of Ash Wednesday,* PB Publishing, Gisborne, Victoria. (Contributors quoted: Rhonda Irving, Rodney Brown, Helen Gibson, Harry Rutherford, Mark Stafford, Sharyn Wade, Frances Wearne)

Reucassel, Craig; 2020, *Big Weather,* ABC Television

Steffensen, Victor; 2020, *Fire Country*, Hardie Grant Travel

Tibbits, Amalie; Handmer, John, et al; 2008, *Community Bushfire Safety,* CSIRO Publications

Victorian Bushfires Royal Commission, 2010, *Final Report Part One & Part Two*, Government Printer, Victoria

Webster, Joan; 2000, *The complete bushfire safety book*, Random House Australia; also available in ebook.

Zinn, Christopher; 2006, 'Survivors remember 1939 Black Friday fires', *ABC News*

Many publications are available. If you need further information, check your local library, and ask for help if you can't find anything related to the subject.

About the author

Bruce Dudon grew up in Shepparton and later moved to Melbourne. He began an optical business in Gisborne in 1980 where he experienced first hand the aftermath of the Ash Wednesday fires for residents. In 1990, he moved to live in Mount Macedon and in 1995, joined the Mount Macedon Fire Brigade. He has since held the positions of Group Training Officer, Communications Officer and Crew Leader. In 2020, Bruce was awarded the 25 Years Service medal.

Bruce has been actively involved in bush fire emergencies, notably during the Blue Mountain fires in 2003 and Black Saturday in 2009. He is passionate about finding ways to help people who live in rural areas to be fire ready.

As a mature age student, Bruce graduated from Victoria University, gaining a Masters in Education. He took up TAFE Sessional Teaching in tourism and business management and worked with student teachers in Hermannsburg and Areyonga. Bruce was a member of the Gisborne Business Association, Macedon Ranges Health, and is presently on the Macedon Ranges Further Education Council.

These days, he enjoys living back in the country on his Woodend acreage.